Pro-Course For Content Marketing Mastery

Creating Engaging Content that Converts and Builds Brands

Aziza Tawfiq Abdelghafar

DEDICATION

For those who dare to dream, persist through challenges, and embrace the journey of lifelong learning. Your resilience shapes the future.

Table of contents

ACKNOWLEDGMENTS

I am deeply grateful to everyone who played a role in bringing this book to life. To my family, whose unwavering support fuels my ambition; to my friends, who inspire and challenge me; and to my mentors and colleagues, whose insights and wisdom have guided my path. Your encouragement has been invaluable.

Thank you for believing in this journey.

About the Book

In today's digital landscape, content isn't just king — it's the entire kingdom. Whether you're an entrepreneur, marketer, or brand builder, mastering the art of content marketing is essential for driving engagement, conversions, and long-term success.

"Pro-Course for Content Marketing Mastery" is a hands-on, step-by-step guide designed to transform you from a content creator into a strategic marketer. This book isn't just theory; it's a practical training course packed with actionable exercises, real-world techniques, and expert insights to help you craft content that doesn't just attract attention — it converts and builds lasting brands.

From understanding the psychology behind compelling messaging to leveraging data-driven optimization, this book covers every stage of the content marketing journey. You'll learn how to:

- **Create content that resonates** with your audience and drives action.

- **Develop a strategic content plan** tailored to your brand's goals.

- **Distribute content effectively** across the right platforms for maximum impact.

- **Measure performance** and refine your approach for continuous growth.

Whether you're looking to sell on Amazon, enhance your marketing skills, or build a powerful brand presence, this book is your ultimate roadmap to content marketing success.

Preface

Great content doesn't happen by accident—it's the result of strategy, creativity, and a deep understanding of what makes your audience tick.

I wrote **"Pro-Course for Content Marketing Mastery"** because I've seen too many businesses and creators struggle with content that falls flat. They pour time and resources into blogs, videos, and social media posts, only to see minimal engagement or conversions. The problem? They're creating content for content's sake, not for impact.

This book is different. It's structured as a **practical, step-by-step course**, blending industry expertise with hands-on exercises to ensure you don't just learn—you apply. Each module builds on the last, guiding you through the fundamentals of content marketing, advanced creation techniques, smart distribution, and performance tracking.

Who is this for?

- **Entrepreneurs** who want to attract and retain customers without relying solely on ads.

- **Marketers** looking to sharpen their content strategy and produce high-converting material.

- **Content creators** ready to move beyond likes and shares to measurable business growth.

- **Brand developers** aiming to build authority and trust in their niche.

By the end of this book, you'll have more than just knowledge —
you'll have a **complete, actionable content marketing
strategy** ready to implement. The digital world rewards those
who communicate effectively. Let's make sure your content
doesn't just speak — it persuades, converts, and grows.

Ready to begin? Let's dive in.

Course Introduction

Content marketing is the backbone of digital success because it's not just about selling—it's about building relationships. In a world where consumers are constantly bombarded with ads and promotions, the only way to stand out is by delivering real value. Content marketing does exactly that. It educates, entertains, and engages your audience so that when they're ready to buy, they think of you first. Unlike traditional advertising, which interrupts and demands attention, content marketing earns trust by being helpful. It's the difference between shouting at your audience and having a meaningful conversation with them.

Many businesses make the mistake of creating promotional content that only talks about their products or services. While this might generate short-term interest, it rarely leads to long-term loyalty. Conversion-driven content, on the other hand, is designed to guide the audience through a journey. It starts by addressing their problems, then offers solutions, and finally presents your brand as the best choice. This type of content doesn't just attract clicks—it builds a connection that turns readers into customers and customers into advocates.

So, what will you learn in this book? You'll discover how to craft content that doesn't just get seen but gets results. You'll learn the psychology behind what makes people engage with certain messages and ignore others. You'll master the art of storytelling so that your brand's message sticks in the minds of your audience. You'll explore different content formats — from blogs and videos to infographics and e-books — and understand which ones work best for your goals. You'll also get hands-on with practical exercises that help you apply what you learn immediately. By the end, you'll have a complete content marketing strategy that you can use to grow your brand, attract more customers, and increase conversions.

This book is for anyone who wants to harness the power of content to drive real business growth. Entrepreneurs will learn how to build a strong online presence without relying solely on paid ads. Marketers will gain advanced techniques to refine their content strategies and maximize ROI. Content creators will move beyond vanity metrics and focus on creating material that actually converts. Brand developers will discover how to establish authority and trust in their industry. Whether you're just starting out or looking to take your skills to the next level, this book gives you the tools to succeed in the competitive world of digital marketing.

Content marketing isn't a trend — it's a fundamental shift in how businesses communicate with their audiences. The old ways of pushing sales messages no longer work. Today, people want authenticity, value, and engagement. They want to feel understood, not sold to. This book will show you how to create content that meets those expectations while still driving measurable business results. You'll learn how to balance creativity with strategy, emotion with logic, and entertainment with education.

One of the biggest challenges in content marketing is consistency. Many brands start strong but lose momentum when they don't see immediate results. This book will teach you how to stay focused on long-term success rather than short-term gains. You'll learn how to repurpose content to get the most out of every piece you create. You'll also discover how to measure performance so you can continuously improve and adapt your strategy.

The digital landscape is always changing, but the principles of great content marketing remain the same. No matter what new platform or algorithm update comes next, the ability to create compelling, valuable content will always be in demand. This book is your guide to mastering those timeless skills while staying adaptable to new trends.

By the time you finish reading, you'll have more than just knowledge — you'll have a clear, actionable plan. You'll know exactly what type of content to create, where to publish it, and how to measure its success. You'll understand how to speak directly to your ideal customers in a way that resonates deeply with them. Most importantly, you'll have the confidence to execute a content strategy that grows your brand and drives real business results.

The journey to content marketing mastery starts here. Whether you're looking to boost your career, grow your business, or simply become a more effective communicator, this book will give you the skills you need. The lessons inside are practical, proven, and designed to deliver real-world results. The only question left is — are you ready to begin?

Module 1: Content Marketing Fundamentals

Let's be honest—jumping into content marketing without understanding the basics is like trying to build a house without a foundation. You might put up some walls, but they won't stand for long. That's why this first module is so important. It's where we lay the groundwork for everything else you'll learn in this book.

Think of content marketing as the art of starting conversations, not just pushing messages. It's about creating something valuable enough that people actually want to engage with it—whether that's reading an article, watching a video, or sharing an infographic. But before you can create content that works, you need to understand why it works.

In this module, we'll break down the core principles that make content marketing so powerful. We'll start by defining what content marketing really is (hint: it's not just blogging) and explore its key goals—like building trust, increasing brand awareness, and attracting the right customers. These aren't just buzzwords; they're the building blocks of a strategy that actually gets results.

Then, we'll dive into the different types of content you can use. Articles, videos, infographics, e-books—each has its own strengths, and knowing which to use (and when) can make all the difference. Finally, we'll walk through the content lifecycle, from the first spark of an idea to publishing and beyond. Because great content isn't just created once; it's optimized, repurposed, and leveraged to keep delivering value.

By the end of this module, you'll have a clear picture of how content marketing fits into the bigger marketing puzzle. You'll also get hands-on with a practical exercise that helps you apply what you've learned right away. No fluff, no theory without application—just actionable insights you can start using immediately.

So, if you've ever wondered why some brands seem to effortlessly attract and engage their audience while others struggle to be heard, this module will give you the answers. Let's get started—your foundation in content marketing begins here.

Lesson 1: Definition and Goals of Content Marketing

Content marketing isn't just about creating posts or publishing articles—it's about building relationships through valuable information. At its core, content marketing is the strategic approach of creating and distributing relevant, useful content to attract and retain a clearly defined audience. Unlike traditional advertising that interrupts people with sales messages, content marketing invites them in by offering something meaningful. It's the difference between shouting from a megaphone and having a genuine conversation.

The real power of content marketing lies in its ability to build trust. In a world where consumers are bombarded with ads and skeptical of brands, trust is the most valuable currency. When you consistently provide helpful information without demanding anything in return, people start seeing you as a reliable source rather than just another company trying to sell them something. This trust transforms casual readers into loyal followers and, eventually, into paying customers. It's a gradual process, but one that creates much stronger customer relationships than any quick sales pitch ever could.

Another fundamental goal of content marketing is increasing brand awareness. Think about how you discovered some of your favorite brands—chances are, it wasn't through a direct advertisement. Maybe you read an insightful blog post, watched an engaging video, or came across an infographic that solved a problem you were having. That's content marketing at work. By creating content that resonates with your target audience, you're putting your brand in front of people when they're most receptive to your message. Over time, this consistent presence makes your brand recognizable and memorable, planting seeds that grow into customer relationships down the line.

Attracting potential customers is where content marketing really shines as a business strategy. Traditional advertising often targets people who may or may not be interested in what you offer. Content marketing, on the other hand, naturally attracts the right people—those who are actively seeking information related to your products or services. When someone finds your content through a Google search or social media share, they're already interested in the topic. This means you're not just reaching more people; you're reaching the right people.

The beauty of content marketing is that it works at every stage of the customer journey. For someone just becoming aware of a problem, your educational content helps them understand their options. For those comparing solutions, your case studies and product comparisons provide the information they need to make decisions. And for existing customers, your ongoing content keeps them engaged and turns them into brand advocates. This full-circle approach is what makes content marketing so effective—it nurtures relationships from first contact to long-term loyalty.

One of the biggest misconceptions about content marketing is that it's just about creating content. The truth is, it's about creating the right content for the right audience at the right time. A beautifully designed infographic won't do much good if it's not answering questions your audience actually has. A comprehensive e-book won't drive results if it's not reaching people who need that information. That's why understanding your audience's needs, challenges, and preferences is so crucial to successful content marketing.

Another key aspect of content marketing is consistency. Unlike advertising campaigns that have clear start and end dates, content marketing is an ongoing process. It's about showing up regularly with valuable information, building that know-like-trust factor over time. This doesn't mean you need to publish content daily, but it does mean maintaining a steady presence that keeps your brand top of mind when your audience is ready to buy.

The goals of content marketing—building trust, increasing awareness, and attracting customers—all work together to create a powerful marketing ecosystem. Trust makes people more receptive to your brand. Awareness ensures they remember you when they need your products or services. And attracting the right potential customers means your marketing efforts are more efficient and effective. When done well, content marketing becomes a self-sustaining system that continues to deliver results long after the content is published.

What makes content marketing particularly valuable in today's digital landscape is its longevity. A single blog post can continue attracting visitors and generating leads months or even years after publication. Compare this to a social media ad that stops working the moment you stop paying for it, and you'll see why so many businesses are investing in content marketing. It's not just a tactic — it's an asset that grows in value over time.

The shift toward content marketing reflects a broader change in consumer behavior. People today want to research and make informed decisions rather than being sold to. They trust peer recommendations and expert advice more than advertising messages. Content marketing aligns perfectly with this preference by positioning your brand as a helpful resource rather than a pushy salesperson. This approach not only feels more authentic to consumers but actually produces better business results in the long run.

Understanding these fundamentals is crucial because everything else in content marketing builds on them. The types of content you create, the platforms you use, the way you measure success — all of these decisions should tie back to these core goals of building trust, increasing awareness, and attracting potential customers. When you keep these objectives in mind, you'll create content that doesn't just look good but actually moves the needle for your business.

As we move through this lesson, remember that effective content marketing isn't about vanity metrics like page views or social media likes. It's about creating genuine connections with your audience that translate into real business growth. Whether you're a solopreneur building your personal brand or a marketing director at a large corporation, these principles remain the same. The scale might change, but the fundamentals don't.

The most successful content marketers aren't necessarily the best writers or the most creative designers—they're the ones who understand how content fits into the bigger picture of business growth. They know how to create material that serves both their audience's needs and their company's goals. This dual focus is what separates effective content marketing from content that just takes up space on the internet.

As you begin developing your own content marketing strategy, keep coming back to these core goals. Ask yourself with every piece of content: Will this build trust with my audience? Will it increase awareness of my brand? Will it attract potential customers? If you can answer yes to at least one of these questions, you're on the right track. If you can answer yes to all three, you've probably got a winning piece of content.

This foundational understanding sets the stage for everything else we'll cover in this book. From choosing content types to distribution strategies to performance measurement, every subsequent lesson ties back to these essential goals. Master these fundamentals, and you'll have a solid base to build all your content marketing efforts upon—one that will serve you well regardless of how algorithms or platforms change in the future.

The digital marketing landscape will continue evolving, but the human desire for valuable, trustworthy information won't. That's why content marketing isn't just another trend—it's a fundamental shift in how businesses communicate with their audiences. By focusing on these core goals, you're not just keeping up with current best practices; you're future-proofing your marketing strategy for whatever changes come next.

Now that we've established what content marketing is and why it matters, we'll explore the different types of content you can use to achieve these goals. But remember—no matter what form your content takes, these fundamental objectives should always guide your strategy. Keep them at the center of your efforts, and you'll create content that truly works for your business.

Lesson 2: Types of Content in Digital Marketing

The digital world offers endless possibilities for content creation, but not all formats work equally well for every purpose. Understanding the different types of content available to you is like having a well-stocked toolbox—you want to reach for the right tool for each specific job. Some content types excel at driving traffic, others at building authority, and some are perfect for nurturing leads through the sales funnel. The key is knowing which type to use when, and how to adapt your message to fit each format naturally.

Articles and blogs form the backbone of most content marketing strategies for good reason. They're versatile, relatively easy to produce, and incredibly effective for search engine visibility. A well-written blog post can continue attracting visitors months or even years after publication, making it one of the most sustainable content investments you can make. The best articles don't just share information—they tell stories, solve problems, and position your brand as a trusted resource. They give you space to dive deep into topics your audience cares about, establishing your expertise while naturally incorporating keywords that help people find you through search.

Videos have exploded in popularity because they're how people increasingly prefer to consume content. There's an intimacy to video that text can't replicate — viewers see your face, hear your voice, and pick up on nonverbal cues that build connection faster than written words alone. Tutorial videos, behind-the-scenes clips, customer testimonials, and live Q&A sessions all create opportunities to engage your audience in more personal ways. Video works particularly well for demonstrating products, explaining complex concepts, or sharing emotional stories that resonate with viewers. Platforms like YouTube serve as search engines for video content, giving your material additional discoverability beyond your own website.

Infographics turn data and complex information into visual stories that are easy to understand and share. Our brains process images much faster than text, making infographics powerful tools for quickly communicating key messages. A well-designed infographic can make statistics memorable, break down processes into clear steps, or compare options in ways that help readers make decisions. They're highly shareable on social media and can drive traffic when other websites embed them with links back to your site. The combination of visual appeal and informational value makes infographics excellent for building brand awareness and establishing thought leadership.

E-books and research reports represent the premium end of content marketing—in-depth resources that provide tremendous value in exchange for contact information. These longer formats allow you to thoroughly explore topics that matter to your audience, positioning your brand as an authority while generating quality leads. An e-book might compile your best insights on an industry challenge, while original research provides data-driven answers to questions your customers are asking. These substantial pieces can be repurposed into multiple blog posts, social media snippets, and presentation material, maximizing your investment in their creation.

Each content type serves different stages of the buyer's journey. Blog posts might attract people at the awareness stage when they're first researching a problem. Videos could engage them as they consider different solutions. E-books and case studies often work best for decision-makers evaluating specific options. The most effective content strategies incorporate multiple formats to guide prospects smoothly from initial curiosity to confident purchasing decisions.

The format you choose should always match your audience's preferences and consumption habits. Younger demographics might prefer quick video tutorials, while professionals in technical fields may value detailed whitepapers. Pay attention to which types of content already perform well in your industry, but don't be afraid to stand out by using formats your competitors neglect. Sometimes the best opportunity lies in creating content in a medium your audience wants but isn't getting from others.

Production quality matters across all content types, but "quality" doesn't necessarily mean expensive. A thoughtfully written blog post with genuine insights outperforms a glossy but shallow article. A simple smartphone video with authentic delivery often connects better than an overproduced corporate piece. Focus first on delivering real value, then upgrade production values as your resources allow. What matters most is that your content resonates with your specific audience — not that it wins design awards.

The most successful content marketers don't limit themselves to one format — they create ecosystems where different content types support and promote each other. A research report becomes a blog post summary, which points to an infographic, which references a video interview. This interconnected approach gives your audience multiple entry points to your content while allowing you to reuse and repurpose material efficiently.

Accessibility should factor into your content format decisions. Videos need captions for hearing-impaired viewers and those watching without sound. Images require alt text descriptions. Text content benefits from clear formatting for easy scanning. Making your content accessible to everyone isn't just good practice — it expands your potential audience and improves your search visibility.

Evergreen content that remains relevant over time forms the foundation of a sustainable strategy, while timely pieces capitalize on current trends and conversations. Blogs and e-books often work well as evergreen resources, while videos and social posts can effectively ride waves of immediate interest. The best content calendars balance both approaches, maintaining consistent value while occasionally joining viral conversations when appropriate for your brand.

Experimentation is key to discovering which content types work best for your unique audience and goals. Try different formats, track their performance, and double down on what delivers results. Many brands find unexpected successes with content types they initially hesitated to try — a law firm might discover their dry subject matter actually makes compelling video content, or a tech company might find their audience loves detailed technical whitepapers.

The content landscape constantly evolves, with new formats emerging regularly. While it's important to stay aware of trends, you don't need to chase every new platform or content type. Focus first on mastering the core formats that align with your audience's needs and your business objectives. Once you have those working well, you can carefully experiment with newer options without spreading your resources too thin.

Remember that great content marketing isn't about using every possible format—it's about using the right formats exceptionally well. A small business might build an entire strategy around excellent blog content and simple explainer videos. A B2B company might focus on in-depth case studies and research reports. What matters is choosing content types that authentically connect with your audience while supporting your business goals.

As you explore different content formats in the coming sections, keep your specific goals in mind. Are you trying to build brand awareness? Establish expertise? Generate leads? Different content types serve different purposes, and the most effective strategies combine them intentionally rather than randomly. The art of content marketing lies in this strategic selection and combination of formats to create a cohesive, compelling narrative about your brand.

Your content mix should also reflect your available resources. It's better to consistently produce one or two types of content well than to struggle with maintaining five or six formats. As you grow more comfortable with content creation and see what resonates, you can gradually expand your repertoire. Many successful content marketers start simple, then layer in additional formats as their confidence and capabilities grow.

The coming lessons will dive deeper into how to create each type of content effectively, but understanding these fundamental differences now will help you make smarter decisions about where to focus your efforts. As you learn more about your audience through research and performance data, you'll be able to refine your content mix to better serve their needs and preferences.

Content marketing succeeds when it feels like a natural conversation rather than a sales pitch. The format you choose should fit the message you want to deliver and the way your audience prefers to receive information. When content type, message, and audience align perfectly, the results can be transformative for your business — building relationships that last far beyond any single piece of content.

Now that we've explored the main content types available to digital marketers, the next step is understanding how to take a piece of content from initial idea through to publication and beyond. The content lifecycle transforms good ideas into strategic assets that work for your business long after their creation date. This ongoing process separates content that gets seen from content that truly performs.

Lesson 3: The Content Lifecycle - From Ideation to Publishing and Optimization

Creating great content isn't a one-time event—it's an ongoing process that begins long before you hit "publish" and continues well after your content goes live. The content lifecycle represents the complete journey of a piece of content from its initial spark of inspiration through to its final optimization, and understanding this cycle is what separates amateur content creators from strategic marketers.

Every successful piece of content starts with a solid idea. But ideation isn't just about coming up with random topics—it's about identifying the specific questions, problems, and interests of your target audience. The best content ideas emerge from genuine insights about what your potential customers actually care about. This might come from customer support interactions, industry forums, social media discussions, or keyword research tools. The key is developing a system for capturing these ideas before they slip away, whether that's a simple spreadsheet, a project management tool, or an old-fashioned notebook.

Once you've identified a promising idea, the next step is research. This is where you dig deeper to understand what's already been said about the topic and where you can add unique value. Look at competing content—not to copy, but to identify gaps you can fill. Maybe others have covered the basics but missed practical applications. Perhaps there's outdated information that needs refreshing. Your goal is to find the angle that makes your content distinct and more valuable than what already exists. This research phase should also uncover relevant data, statistics, and examples that will strengthen your content's authority and usefulness.

With research complete, planning comes next. This is where you determine the best format for your content based on the topic complexity, audience preferences, and your marketing goals. A complex how-to guide might work best as a video tutorial or step-by-step article. A data-heavy subject could shine as an infographic or research report. During planning, you'll also outline the structure of your content, identifying key sections, subtopics, and the logical flow that will guide your audience through the material. A well-structured outline serves as your roadmap, making the actual creation process smoother and more efficient.

Content creation is where your planning comes to life, but it's important to remember that perfectionism can be the enemy of progress. The first draft doesn't need to be flawless — it just needs to exist. Many content creators find it helpful to separate the writing/creation process from the editing process. Get your ideas down first, then refine them later. This approach keeps the creative flow moving forward without getting bogged down in endless tweaks. Depending on your content type, creation might involve writing, filming, designing, or recording — but in all cases, the focus should remain on delivering clear value to your audience.

Editing transforms your rough draft into polished content. This stage goes beyond just fixing typos — it's about sharpening your message, improving clarity, and ensuring your content achieves its intended purpose. Good editing makes complex ideas simple, cuts unnecessary fluff, and ensures your content speaks in a consistent brand voice. Many creators benefit from having a second set of eyes review their work, as fresh perspectives often catch issues the original creator might miss. Editing also includes optimizing your content for search engines by naturally incorporating relevant keywords, writing compelling meta descriptions, and ensuring proper formatting for readability.

Before publishing comes preparation — getting all the supporting elements in place. This includes creating engaging headlines that grab attention while accurately representing the content, selecting or creating appropriate images that enhance understanding, and preparing social media snippets to promote the content. You'll also want to consider any calls-to-action that will guide readers toward the next step you want them to take, whether that's subscribing to your email list, downloading a related resource, or exploring your products. These elements turn your content from passive information into an active part of your marketing funnel.

Publishing might seem like the finish line, but in the content lifecycle, it's really just the beginning of the next phase. Where and how you publish matters tremendously. The same piece of content might need slight adaptations for different platforms — a blog post on your website, a condensed version on LinkedIn, key takeaways as Twitter threads, or visual snippets for Instagram. Each platform has its own best practices for optimal presentation and engagement. Timing also plays a role — publishing when your audience is most active increases initial visibility and engagement.

After publication comes promotion — actively getting your content in front of the right eyes. This might involve sharing across your social channels, including it in your email newsletter, reaching out to influencers who might find it valuable, or even running targeted ads to boost visibility. Many great pieces of content fail simply because no one knows they exist. Promotion ensures your hard work gets the attention it deserves. Building relationships with others in your industry can lead to organic sharing of your content, while strategic partnerships can help amplify your reach.

Monitoring performance is how you learn what's working and what isn't. Tools like Google Analytics show you how people are finding and interacting with your content. Are they reading to the end? Which sections keep their attention? Where do they drop off? Social platforms provide their own insights into shares, likes, and comments. This data isn't just numbers — it's direct feedback about what resonates with your audience. Establishing key performance indicators (KPIs) before publishing helps you measure success objectively rather than relying on gut feelings.

Optimization is the phase where you improve existing content based on performance data and changing information. Maybe a blog post needs updating with newer statistics. Perhaps a video could benefit from additional examples based on viewer questions. Optimization might involve tweaking headlines for better click-through rates, adding internal links to newer relevant content, or refreshing metadata to improve search visibility. Evergreen content — material that remains relevant over time — benefits greatly from regular optimization to maintain its value and performance.

Repurposing extends the value of your content by adapting it for different formats and uses. A comprehensive blog post might become a series of social media graphics. A webinar recording could be edited into shorter tutorial videos. Research findings might transform into an infographic. Repurposing isn't about being lazy — it's about meeting your audience where they are with the content formats they prefer. It also helps reinforce your key messages through repetition across different channels.

The final phase of the content lifecycle is retirement — knowing when to remove or archive content that's no longer accurate or helpful. Outdated content can harm your credibility and even hurt your search rankings if it provides poor user experience. Some content can be updated and republished, while others may need to be removed entirely with proper redirects put in place. Regular content audits help identify which pieces need refreshing, which should be retired, and which continue performing well.

Understanding this complete lifecycle changes how you approach content creation. Instead of viewing each piece as a standalone project, you begin to see how content works together as a system — how one piece can lead to another, how older content supports newer efforts, and how different formats can work together to tell a complete story. This systemic view helps you work smarter, not harder, getting more value from each piece of content you create.

The most successful content marketers don't just create — they nurture their content over time, helping it grow and adapt just like a living thing. They track performance, listen to audience feedback, and make continuous improvements. This ongoing attention is what transforms good content into exceptional content that consistently delivers results long after its initial publication.

Practical Exercise: Choose a product or service and define two suitable content types for it. Think through how each would progress through the complete content lifecycle—from initial idea to ongoing optimization. Consider how you would repurpose each piece to extend its value and reach. This exercise will help you develop the strategic thinking needed to make your content work harder for your business.

Remember, mastering the content lifecycle isn't about doing more work—it's about working more strategically. When you understand and implement each phase effectively, your content becomes a powerful asset that continues delivering value long after the initial effort of creation. This is the key to building a sustainable content marketing strategy that grows with your business.

Practical Exercise: Content Type Selection

Let's put what you've learned into practice. Imagine you're working with a local fitness studio that offers personalized training programs and nutrition coaching. Your task is to select two content types that would effectively market their services while aligning with the goals of building trust, increasing awareness, and attracting potential clients.

For the first content type, an **educational video series** would work exceptionally well. These could be short 3-5 minute clips demonstrating proper exercise techniques, explaining common form mistakes, or showing quick workout routines people can do at home. Videos allow the trainers to showcase their expertise while building trust through their physical presence and teaching ability. The studio could post these on YouTube (for search visibility) and Instagram (for community engagement), using them to establish authority in fitness training while naturally highlighting their personalized approach. Each video could end with a soft call-to-action inviting viewers to learn more about their customized programs.

The second ideal content type would be **client transformation case studies** presented as blog posts with before/after photos and interview quotes. These narrative-driven pieces would follow real clients through their fitness journeys, detailing their specific challenges, how the studio's program addressed them, and the measurable results achieved. Case studies build tremendous social proof and trust while demonstrating the studio's unique value proposition. They can be repurposed into social media snippets, email newsletter features, and even printed materials in the studio itself. For maximum impact, each case study would include a section where the trainers explain the science behind their approach, further establishing their expertise.

This combination works because:

1. The videos attract broad interest through helpful, searchable content

2. The case studies convert interest into leads by showing proven results

3. Together they cover both top-of-funnel (awareness) and middle-of-funnel (consideration) content needs

4. Both formats allow the studio's personality and training philosophy to shine through

Now it's your turn. Choose either:
A) An eco-friendly cleaning product line
B) A financial planning service for young professionals
C) Your own business or a company you're familiar with

For your selected product/service:

1. Identify two content types that would effectively market it

2. Explain why each format suits this particular business

3. Describe how each piece would support the core content marketing goals

4. Suggest one platform where each content type would perform best

This exercise helps bridge the gap between theory and practice, ensuring you can apply content marketing fundamentals to real-world scenarios. Remember - the best content choices always stem from understanding both the business offering and the target audience's needs.

Module 2: Strategies for Creating Impactful Content

Let's be honest — creating content is easy. Creating content that actually works? That's where the real challenge begins.

In Module 1, we laid the foundation by understanding what content marketing is and exploring different content types. Now, we're moving from "what" to "how" — how to create content that doesn't just exist, but performs. Content that grabs attention, builds connections, and drives action.

This module is where strategy meets creativity. We'll start by getting inside your audience's head (Lesson 1), because great content begins with deep understanding, not assumptions. You'll learn how to create detailed buyer personas and identify the real pain points that keep your audience up at night.

Then we'll tackle the blank page problem (Lesson 2). That moment when you're staring at an empty document, wondering what to write about. You'll discover proven brainstorming techniques and powerful tools to generate endless content ideas that actually resonate with your audience.

Finally, we'll focus on crafting messages that stick (Lesson 3). Because it's not just what you say — it's how you say it. You'll learn the art of writing headlines that demand to be clicked, adapting your tone to match your audience's expectations, and using storytelling to make your content memorable and shareable.

The practical task at the end will challenge you to apply these lessons immediately. You'll craft a compelling headline and outline key points for an article—exactly the kind of real-world skill you need in content marketing.

Here's the truth: In a world where everyone is creating content, the winners are those who create with purpose, precision, and psychological understanding. That's what this module will help you achieve.

Ready to move beyond basic content creation and start developing truly impactful material? Let's begin.

Lesson 1: Knowing Your Target Audience

Creating content without understanding your audience is like throwing darts in the dark—you might hit something by chance, but you'll waste a lot of effort missing the mark. The most successful content marketers know their audience so well they can almost predict what questions they'll ask next. This deep understanding doesn't come from guesswork—it comes from developing detailed buyer personas and identifying real pain points that keep your potential customers up at night.

Buyer personas are fictional representations of your ideal customers, based on real data and research. They go beyond basic demographics to capture motivations, challenges, and decision-making processes. A well-crafted persona might include details like "Sarah, 34, marketing manager at a mid-sized tech company who struggles to prove ROI on content efforts" rather than just "female, 30-40, works in marketing." The difference between these two approaches determines whether your content resonates or falls flat. Creating these personas starts with asking the right questions—what keeps them up at night? What are their professional aspirations? How do they prefer to consume information? What objections might they have to your solution?

The process of building accurate personas requires looking at multiple data sources. Customer interviews provide qualitative insights you can't get from analytics alone. Sales teams often have invaluable information about common objections and questions from prospects. Website analytics show what content your audience already engages with. Social media listening reveals what they're talking about in their own words. Even customer support logs can uncover frequent problems people encounter. Combining these sources creates a multidimensional view of who you're creating content for and why they care.

Pain points represent the specific problems your audience wants to solve—the aches in their professional or personal lives that keep recurring. These aren't surface-level complaints but deeper frustrations that influence decisions. For a small business owner, it might not just be "I need more customers" but "I don't have time to learn new marketing tactics while running daily operations." For a new parent, it might not just be "I need baby clothes" but "I want organic materials but can't afford premium brands." Identifying these nuanced pain points allows you to create content that speaks directly to real struggles rather than generic topics.

Interests complement pain points by revealing what excites and motivates your audience beyond their challenges. These might include professional development goals, personal aspirations, or industry trends they follow. A financial advisor's audience might be interested in early retirement strategies not just because they worry about savings, but because they dream of traveling the world. Tapping into these positive motivations can make your content more inspiring and shareable while still addressing core needs.

The intersection of pain points and interests is where the most powerful content lives. This is where you solve problems while connecting to bigger aspirations — helping someone overcome an immediate obstacle while moving toward a larger goal. Content that addresses both dimensions creates deeper engagement because it speaks to the whole person, not just one aspect of their needs.

Understanding your audience's content consumption habits is equally important. Some audiences prefer quick video tutorials they can watch during lunch breaks. Others want comprehensive guides they can bookmark and reference. Professionals in regulated industries might prioritize authoritative whitepapers, while creative entrepreneurs might engage more with visual case studies. These preferences influence everything from content format to length to publishing schedule.

Language and communication style matter just as much as content type. The way you explain concepts to tech-savvy early adopters will differ from how you communicate with less technical audiences. Industry jargon can establish credibility with some readers while alienating others. Even something as simple as sentence length and paragraph structure should adapt to your audience's reading preferences — busy executives might prefer skimmable bullet points while academics expect more nuanced discussions.

Psychological triggers play a significant role in audience engagement. Some people respond strongly to content that emphasizes security and risk reduction. Others are motivated by opportunities for growth and achievement. Understanding these underlying drivers helps craft messages that resonate emotionally, not just logically. This doesn't mean manipulating your audience—it means communicating in ways they naturally find compelling and authentic.

The buyer's journey—awareness, consideration, decision—requires different content approaches at each stage. Early-stage content educates about problems and establishes your expertise. Middle-stage content compares solutions and addresses objections. Late-stage content provides the final push toward choosing your offering. Mapping your content to these stages ensures you meet audiences where they are rather than jumping straight to sales messages they're not ready for.

Audience research should be ongoing, not a one-time exercise. Preferences evolve, new challenges emerge, and market conditions shift. Regularly updating your personas and pain point analysis keeps your content relevant as these changes occur. This might involve quarterly surveys, monitoring industry forums, or tracking which existing content performs best over time.

Competitor audience analysis can reveal gaps and opportunities. See what questions go unanswered in their comment sections. Note which of their content pieces generate the most engagement. Look for audience segments they might be overlooking. This isn't about copying competitors but identifying unmet needs you can address better.

Creating audience empathy bridges the gap between data and compelling content. When you can genuinely put yourself in your audience's shoes — understanding their daily frustrations, professional pressures, and personal aspirations — your content naturally becomes more helpful and engaging. This empathy comes through in word choice, examples used, and problems addressed, making your audience feel truly understood rather than just marketed to.

The most effective content marketers blend analytical and creative thinking when understanding their audience. They back up instincts with data while interpreting data with human insight. They recognize patterns in behavior while remembering that behind every data point is a real person with unique needs. This balanced approach prevents content from becoming either too clinical or too generic.

Validating your audience assumptions is crucial before investing heavily in content creation. Small tests — like social media polls or simple blog posts — can confirm whether you've correctly identified pain points and interests before developing more substantial content assets. This validation saves time and resources while refining your understanding.

Segmenting your broader audience into smaller groups allows for more targeted content. Not all customers have identical needs, and trying to speak to everyone often means resonating deeply with no one. Creating content clusters for different segments — while maintaining overall brand consistency — increases relevance and effectiveness.

Cultural context influences how audiences perceive and engage with content. Regional differences, industry norms, and company cultures all shape what content approaches work best. A casual, humorous tone might work for some audiences while others expect more formal communication. Understanding these nuances prevents missteps and strengthens connection.

The ultimate test of audience understanding is whether your content sparks action. When you truly know your audience, your content doesn't just get consumed—it gets shared, saved, and acted upon. It moves people through their buyer's journey naturally because it meets them where they are with what they need.

Practical Exercise:
Choose a product or service you're familiar with. Conduct basic audience research by:

1. Identifying three key buyer personas

2. Listing five primary pain points for each

3. Noting three core interests for each

4. Describing their preferred content formats
    This exercise builds the foundation for all content you'll create—getting the audience right makes everything else easier.

Remember: Great content begins with great audience understanding. The time invested in developing detailed personas and identifying real pain points pays off in content that converts casual browsers into engaged followers and loyal customers. When you know your audience this well, creating content they love becomes not just easier, but almost instinctive.

Lesson 2: Content Ideation Techniques

Coming up with fresh content ideas consistently is one of the biggest challenges marketers face. That blank page staring back at you can feel intimidating, but with the right techniques and tools, you'll never run out of compelling topics that resonate with your audience. Content ideation isn't about waiting for inspiration to strike—it's about having reliable systems to generate ideas on demand while keeping your finger on the pulse of what your audience truly cares about.

Brainstorming works best when approached systematically rather than randomly. One powerful technique is the "question storm" method where you generate as many questions as possible that your audience might have about your topic. For a financial advisor, this could range from "How much should I save for retirement?" to "What investments perform well during inflation?" These questions become instant content ideas that address real information needs. Another approach is the "content cluster" method where you identify pillar topics (broad main subjects) and then brainstorm numerous related subtopics. A home improvement business might have "kitchen remodeling" as a pillar topic, with subtopics like "budget-friendly cabinet upgrades" or "maximizing small kitchen spaces."

Mind mapping visually organizes ideas in a way that sparks new connections. Start with a central topic in the middle of a page, then branch out with related themes, questions, formats, and angles. The visual nature often reveals content opportunities you might miss with linear lists. For example, a central topic of "remote work" could branch into productivity tools, home office setups, team communication challenges, and work-life balance tips — each with their own subtopics worth exploring.

The "5 Ws and H" framework (Who, What, When, Where, Why, How) forces you to examine topics from multiple perspectives. A pet supply store could create content around "Who benefits most from grain-free diets?" "What are signs your dog needs different food?" "When should you transition puppy to adult food?" etc. This simple structure consistently generates fresh angles on even well-covered topics.

Reverse brainstorming starts by identifying content you don't want to create — generic, salesy, or superficial material — then defining the opposite characteristics. If "10% discount on our products" is uninspiring content, its opposite might be "How to choose the right [product] for your specific needs" — a much more valuable piece. This technique helps avoid common content traps while steering toward more engaging approaches.

Customer journey mapping reveals content opportunities at each stage of the buyer's path. Awareness stage content educates about problems ("Signs your small business needs better cash flow management"). Consideration stage content compares solutions ("Invoice factoring vs business loans"). Decision stage content helps finalize choices ("Questions to ask before choosing a factoring company"). Mapping these needs ensures your content covers the full spectrum rather than clustering around one stage.

Social listening involves monitoring online conversations for emerging questions and concerns. Industry forums, Facebook groups, Twitter threads, and Reddit discussions are goldmines for unfiltered audience pain points. Notice recurring questions and language patterns — these become your content blueprints. When multiple people ask some variation of "How do I..." or "Why does..." you've found proven content topics.

AnswerThePublic transforms seed keywords into visual maps of actual search queries. Entering "yoga" might reveal questions like "yoga for back pain" or "yoga vs pilates for weight loss" — each representing specific content opportunities. The tool organizes queries by question words (what, how, can), prepositions (for, with, near), and comparisons, giving you dozens of content angles from a single keyword. Seeing these search patterns helps you anticipate and answer the exact questions people are asking.

Semrush's Topic Research tool provides comprehensive data on what content performs well for any given topic. It shows popular headlines, questions people ask, and related searches — all valuable for ideation. The "Content Gap" feature identifies keywords competitors rank for that you don't, revealing overlooked content opportunities. These insights ensure your content ideas are data-driven rather than guesswork.

Google's "People also ask" boxes and autocomplete suggestions reveal related queries in real-time. Start typing your main topic in Google and note the predictive searches — these reflect actual search volume. Clicking on a "People also ask" question triggers new related questions to appear, creating an endless chain of content ideas based on genuine user intent.

Industry reports and academic studies provide data-rich content opportunities. Look for surprising statistics or counterintuitive findings that challenge common assumptions — "Study shows 68% of small businesses overpay for [service]" makes a compelling headline. These authoritative sources lend credibility while offering fresh perspectives on familiar topics.

Competitor content analysis (done ethically) shows what resonates in your space. Note which of their pieces have high engagement, then consider how you could create something more comprehensive, updated, or from a different angle. The goal isn't to copy but to identify content needs they haven't fully addressed.

Seasonal and trending topics provide timely content hooks. Tools like Google Trends show rising search interest, while holiday calendars suggest relevant tie-ins. A tax preparer might create content around "Quarterly estimated tax deadlines" or "Year-end tax planning moves." These timely pieces often gain temporary but significant traffic boosts.

Customer feedback and FAQs are direct lines to content needs. Support tickets, sales call transcripts, and email inquiries reveal exactly what information people struggle to find. Turning common questions into content prevents repetitive inquiries while positioning you as helpful and attentive.

Product or service features translate naturally into how-to content. Each aspect of what you offer can spawn multiple pieces — not just "Our CRM features" but "How [feature] solves [specific pain point]." This approach demonstrates value while educating potential customers.

The best content ideas often come from combining multiple techniques — using brainstorming to generate raw ideas, then tools like AnswerThePublic to validate search interest, and finally competitor analysis to spot gaps. This multi-method approach ensures your content is creative yet data-backed, original yet proven to resonate.

Practical Task:
Take one of your products/services and:

1. Generate 10 content ideas using the question storm method

2. Find 5 additional angles using AnswerThePublic or Semrush

3. Identify 3 seasonal/trending opportunities
   This systematic approach guarantees you'll never lack for compelling content topics that drive real results.

Remember: Consistent content ideation isn't about random creativity—it's about having reliable processes to uncover what your audience truly wants to know. When you combine structured brainstorming with data-driven tools, you create content that's both imaginative and impactful.

Lesson 3: Crafting the Right Message

The difference between content that gets ignored and content that gets results often comes down to how the message is crafted. You could have the most valuable information in the world, but if it's not packaged in a way that grabs attention and resonates emotionally, it might as well not exist. This lesson breaks down the three essential elements of powerful messaging: headlines that demand to be read, tone that connects personally, and stories that stick in memory long after the content is consumed.

Compelling headlines act as the front door to your content. In our information-overloaded world, you have about three seconds to convince someone your content is worth their time. The best headlines do this by promising a clear benefit, triggering curiosity, or speaking directly to the reader's identity. There's science behind what makes headlines work—specific numbers perform better than vague quantities, emotional words increase shares, and questions often drive higher click-through rates. But beyond formulas, great headlines reflect a deep understanding of what your audience truly cares about. They focus on the reader's gain rather than your product's features. "How to Reduce Your Energy Bills by 30% Without Replacing Windows" works better than "Our Window Installation Services" because it leads with the outcome rather than the offering.

Headlines also need to match the content format and platform. A YouTube video title might include brackets like [Step-by-Step Tutorial] because viewers search for specific formats. LinkedIn article headlines often perform better when they hint at professional insights or career benefits. The same core message gets adjusted based on where and how it will be consumed. Testing different headline variations is crucial—sometimes changing just one word can double engagement. Tools like CoSchedule's Headline Analyzer provide instant feedback on emotional impact and readability, while A/B testing reveals what actually works with your specific audience.

Adapting tone and language to your audience is about more than just professionalism versus casualness. It's about mirroring how your audience thinks and talks about their challenges. A financial advisor targeting retirees will use different language than one targeting young crypto investors, even when explaining similar concepts. This adaptation goes beyond vocabulary to include sentence structure, cultural references, and even humor appropriateness. The tone should align with both your brand personality and your audience's expectations—you wouldn't use slapstick humor when discussing funeral services, nor stiff formality when teaching kids' crafts.

Reading level matters more than many creators realize. Unless you're writing for academics, simpler language typically performs better. The Hemingway Editor helps identify complex sentences and passive voice that might create unnecessary friction. This doesn't mean dumbing down content — it means removing barriers to understanding so your valuable insights can shine through. Industry jargon should be used strategically — enough to establish credibility with insiders but not so much that it alienates newcomers. When technical terms are necessary, quick explanations or links to definitions keep the content accessible.

Storytelling transforms abstract concepts into memorable experiences. Our brains are wired to remember stories far better than facts alone. In content marketing, stories typically follow one of several proven structures: the hero's journey (how someone overcame a challenge), before-and-after transformations, or day-in-the-life scenarios that build empathy. What makes these stories effective isn't just the narrative arc but the specific, sensory details that make them feel real. "Our software increased productivity" is forgettable; "Sarah regained 11 hours per week previously lost to manual data entry" sticks because it's concrete and human.

The most effective marketing stories position the customer as the hero, not your brand. Your product or service should play the role of guide or tool that helps them succeed. This subtle shift in perspective makes stories far more relatable and less salesy. Case studies become powerful when they focus on the customer's emotional journey — not just the features they used but how those features made them feel and what they could finally achieve.

Practical Task:

Write a headline for a marketing article about time management for small business owners, then outline three key points the article would cover. Make sure the headline follows best practices while the points reflect real pain points your audience faces. This exercise bridges the gap between understanding messaging principles and applying them to actual content creation.

Remember: Crafting the right message isn't about manipulation—it's about removing friction between your valuable ideas and the audience that needs them. When you master headlines, tone adaptation, and storytelling, your content doesn't just communicate—it connects, persuades, and inspires action. These skills transform good content into content that truly works for your business.

Practical Task: Crafting a Compelling Marketing Article

Headline:
"5 Time-Saving Hacks Every Small Business Owner Wishes They Knew Sooner"

Three Key Points:

1. **The Hidden Time Thieves in Your Daily Routine**

   o Identifying common productivity drains (excessive meetings, email overload, multitasking)

   o How tracking your time for one week reveals surprising inefficiencies

   o The 80/20 rule applied to small business tasks

2. **Automation Tools That Actually Save Time (Without the Learning Curve)**

   o 3 affordable tools for automating invoicing, social media, and customer follow-ups

   o How to implement one automation at a time without overwhelm

   o Real examples from local businesses saving 5+ hours weekly

3. **The Delegation Mindset: Doing Less to Achieve More**

   o Breaking the "I need to do everything myself" mentality

   o What tasks to outsource first (and how to find reliable help)

○ Calculating the true cost of your time versus delegation costs

Why This Works:

- The headline uses curiosity ("wishes they knew sooner") and promises specific, actionable value

- Each point addresses a different aspect of time management (awareness, tools, mindset)

- Provides concrete numbers and examples to establish credibility

- Focuses on emotional pain points (frustration, overwhelm) while offering practical solutions

Bonus   Tip:
This structure easily adapts to multiple content formats:

- Blog post with tool screenshots

- Video demonstrating the automation tools

- Infographic comparing time spent vs. time saved

- Twitter thread breaking down each hack

Module 3: Publishing and Distributing Content Effectively

You've done the hard work - researched your audience, crafted compelling content, and polished your message. Now comes the make-or-break moment: getting your content seen by the right people at the right time. This module is where great content meets strategic distribution, because even the most brilliant piece will fail if it doesn't reach its intended audience.

Think of this module as your content amplification playbook. We'll start by helping you choose the right platforms (Lesson 1) - because spraying your content everywhere is just as ineffective as keeping it locked away. You'll learn how to match different content types with the platforms where your audience actually spends time, whether that's LinkedIn for B2B professionals or Instagram for visual storytelling.

Then we'll tackle the art and science of timing (Lesson 2). You'll discover how scheduling tools can save you hours while maximizing engagement, and learn smart repetition techniques that keep your content working without becoming annoying. We'll also cover the content repurposing strategies that top marketers use to squeeze maximum value from every piece they create.

Finally, we'll address the often-overlooked but crucial element of collaboration (Lesson 3). Whether you're working with an in-house team or external creators, maintaining brand consistency while encouraging creativity is essential. You'll learn how to develop practical style guides that actually get used, not just filed away.

The practical exercise will have you designing a two-week editorial calendar - the exact kind of real-world skill that separates professional content marketers from hobbyists. You'll make strategic decisions about what to publish when, and how different pieces can work together to tell a cohesive story.

Here's the truth: Distribution isn't just the last step in content marketing - it's what makes all your other efforts worthwhile. By the end of this module, you'll have a clear system to ensure your hard work gets the attention it deserves, reaching the people who need it most.

Ready to move beyond creation and master the art of getting your content seen? Let's begin.

Lesson 1: Choosing the Right Platforms

The digital landscape offers countless places to share your content, but trying to be everywhere at once is a recipe for burnout and mediocre results. Smart content marketers understand that platform selection is about strategic focus rather than blanket coverage. Each platform serves different purposes, reaches distinct audiences, and requires tailored approaches to maximize impact. Let's examine the three core platforms that form the foundation of most successful content distribution strategies.

Blogs represent your owned media real estate - the one place online where you have complete control over your content and messaging. Unlike social platforms that can change algorithms overnight or email services that control your access to subscribers, your blog remains your permanent home base. The beauty of blog content lies in its longevity. A well-optimized blog post can continue attracting visitors and generating leads months or even years after publication, making it one of the most sustainable marketing assets you can create. Blogs excel at establishing thought leadership through in-depth articles that showcase your expertise. They provide the space to thoroughly explain complex topics, answer common customer questions, and demonstrate your unique perspective on industry issues. From an SEO perspective, blogs help you capture valuable search traffic by targeting specific keywords your audience uses when researching solutions. The key to successful blogging is consistency - both in publishing frequency and in delivering value that keeps readers coming back. A blog also serves as the hub for all your other content distribution, providing a destination where you can convert visitors into email subscribers or leads.

Social media platforms like LinkedIn, Instagram, and Twitter function as your content amplification channels - the places where you engage in industry conversations and build relationships at scale. Each platform has its own personality and best practices. LinkedIn thrives on professional insights and career-focused content, making it ideal for B2B marketers and service providers. The platform rewards content that sparks thoughtful discussion among professionals, with long-form posts performing particularly well. Instagram's visual nature makes it perfect for brands with strong aesthetics or those selling physical products. The platform's various formats - feed posts, stories, reels - allow for creative storytelling that can showcase your brand personality. Twitter's fast-paced environment suits timely commentary, quick tips, and participation in trending industry conversations. The common thread across all social platforms is the need for authentic engagement rather than pure broadcasting. Social media works best when you focus on building communities rather than just pushing content. This means responding to comments, participating in relevant discussions, and creating content that encourages sharing and interaction. The ephemeral nature of social content means you'll need to post frequently to stay visible, but the payoff comes in increased brand awareness and website traffic.

Email marketing remains one of the most powerful distribution channels because it reaches people who have already expressed interest in your brand. Unlike social algorithms that decide who sees your content, email goes directly to subscribers' inboxes - assuming it avoids spam filters. Email excels at nurturing relationships over time through regular, valuable communication. Newsletters can repurpose your best blog content while adding exclusive insights for subscribers. Drip campaigns automatically deliver targeted content based on subscriber actions or characteristics. Transactional emails provide helpful information alongside purchase confirmations or account updates. The key to effective email marketing is segmentation - sending the right content to the right people at the right time. A new subscriber might receive a welcome sequence introducing your brand's core concepts, while a long-time customer might get advanced tips or loyalty offers. Email also provides some of the clearest metrics for measuring content performance, with open rates and click-through rates offering immediate feedback on what resonates with your audience. Unlike social platforms where organic reach has declined, email maintains strong deliverability when you focus on providing consistent value to engaged subscribers.

The art of platform selection involves matching your content types with the platforms where they'll perform best. A detailed industry report makes more sense as a blog post or LinkedIn article than as a series of tweets. A product demonstration might shine on Instagram but fall flat in an email newsletter. Consider both the format of your content and the mindset of users on each platform. LinkedIn users typically browse in professional mode, seeking career insights and business solutions. Instagram users often scroll for entertainment and inspiration. Email subscribers have explicitly opted in to hear from you, making them more receptive to detailed content. The platform also determines how you adapt your messaging. The same core idea might become a long-form blog post, a carousel of Instagram slides, a Twitter thread, and an email summary - each version tailored to the platform's norms and user expectations.

Understanding platform strengths helps you allocate your limited time and resources effectively. A common mistake is spreading efforts too thinly across too many platforms. It's better to dominate one or two key channels than to have a lackluster presence everywhere. Start by identifying where your ideal audience spends the most time and which platforms best showcase your content strengths. A consultant might focus on LinkedIn and email, while a fashion brand might prioritize Instagram and their blog. As you gain traction on your core platforms, you can carefully expand to others with a clear strategy for each. Every piece of content should have a primary platform where it makes the most impact, with other platforms used to amplify and repurpose that content. This hub-and-spoke approach ensures your best work gets maximum visibility without requiring you to create unique content for every channel.

Platform selection also depends on your marketing funnel. Blogs and social media excel at top-of-funnel awareness, attracting new audiences through search and discovery. Email works best for middle- and bottom-of-funnel nurturing, moving subscribers closer to purchase decisions. Your platform mix should reflect where you need the most impact - whether that's reaching new audiences, engaging existing followers, or driving conversions. Over time, you'll develop a content ecosystem where each platform plays a specific role in attracting, engaging, and converting your ideal customers. The most effective content marketers don't just create great content - they understand exactly where that content will deliver the most value and how different platforms work together to move audiences through the buyer's journey.

Lesson 2: Scheduling and Smart Repetition

Creating great content is only half the battle - the real magic happens when you strategically schedule and repurpose that content to maximize its reach and impact. In today's fast-paced digital landscape, even your best work can get lost in the noise if you don't have a smart distribution plan. This lesson will transform how you think about content scheduling and repurposing, turning single pieces of content into multi-format assets that work harder for your business.

Scheduling tools like Buffer and Later are game-changers for content marketers. These platforms do much more than just automate posts - they provide a centralized command center for all your content distribution. Buffer's intuitive interface makes it easy to queue up content across multiple social platforms while maintaining each network's unique formatting requirements. The analytics dashboard shows you exactly which posts perform best, helping you refine your strategy over time. Later specializes in visual platforms like Instagram, with features that let you preview exactly how your grid will look before you post. Both tools offer optimal timing suggestions based on when your specific audience is most active online. The real power comes from batching your scheduling work - setting aside dedicated time to plan and queue content rather than scrambling to post in real-time. This approach ensures consistency (which algorithms reward) while freeing up your mental energy for content creation and engagement.

Smart repetition is the secret weapon most marketers overlook. The reality is that most of your audience will never see a piece of content the first time you share it. Strategic reposting allows you to get more mileage from your best work without coming across as spammy. The key is varying the framing - share the same blog post with different quotes, ask new discussion questions each time, or highlight different takeaways. Evergreen content can be reshared every few months, while timely pieces might have a shorter but more intense promotion window. Tools like MeetEdgar take this further by automatically cycling through your content library, ensuring your archive keeps working for you. This doesn't mean being repetitive - it means giving valuable content multiple chances to reach people at the exact moment they need it.

Content repurposing is where the real efficiency gains happen. A single comprehensive blog post can become:

- A Twitter thread breaking down key points

- An infographic summarizing main takeaways

- A LinkedIn article expanding on one specific aspect

- A YouTube video discussing the concepts

- Multiple Instagram carousel posts

- An email newsletter segment

- A podcast episode

The art lies in adapting the content for each format's strengths rather than just copying and pasting. A technical whitepaper becomes an accessible explainer video. A data-heavy report transforms into bite-sized social media statistics with visual appeal. This pyramid approach to content creation means you invest serious effort in one cornerstone piece, then efficiently adapt it for multiple channels. Not only does this save time, but it reinforces your message through multiple touchpoints - crucial for breaking through today's content clutter.

Seasonal content deserves special attention in your scheduling strategy. That brilliant holiday gift guide or tax season checklist should be dusted off and re-promoted when relevant each year. Create calendar reminders to update and re-share these perennial performers, adding fresh examples or current data to keep them feeling timely. This approach gives you reliable content anchors throughout the year while requiring minimal new creation.

The most effective content marketers view scheduling as part of the creative process, not just an administrative task. When you know how and when content will be distributed, you can create with that context in mind. A blog post can be written with pull-quotes ready for social sharing. Videos can be edited with platform-specific formats in mind. This forward-thinking approach makes the scheduling and repurposing process seamless rather than an afterthought.

Practical Exercise:
Take one of your existing blog posts or videos and:

1. Identify three different ways to repurpose it for other platforms

2. Create a scheduling plan that shares it multiple times over two months

3. Outline how you would adapt the messaging for each repurposed version

This exercise will help you develop the strategic mindset needed to maximize every piece of content you create. Remember - in content marketing, efficiency isn't about doing less work, it's about getting more results from the work you do. Smart scheduling and repurposing let you maintain a consistent presence without constantly creating from scratch.

Lesson 3: Collaborating with Teams and Creators

Consistency is the secret ingredient that transforms random content into a recognizable brand experience. When multiple people contribute to your content—whether in-house team members or external creators—maintaining a unified voice becomes both crucial and challenging. This lesson breaks down the systems that keep everyone aligned, ensuring your content feels cohesive no matter who creates it or where it appears.

A living style guide serves as your brand's content bible—but unlike traditional style guides that collect dust, this should be an active, evolving document. Start by defining your brand personality traits (are you friendly and approachable or authoritative and professional?) and translate these into writing guidelines. Include specifics like sentence length preferences, paragraph structure, and how to handle industry jargon. For visual content, establish standards for color palettes, image styles, and graphic treatments. The most effective guides provide concrete examples of what to do—and what to avoid—with clear before/after samples that illustrate your standards in action.

Voice consistency goes deeper than word choice—it's about maintaining the same underlying perspective and values across all content. If your brand takes an educational rather than salesy approach, this should shine through whether you're writing a tweet or producing a video. Develop a "brand character" exercise where contributors imagine your brand as a person—how would they explain complex topics at a dinner party? What jokes would they tell (or avoid)? This mental model helps diverse creators channel the same authentic voice.

Collaboration tools streamline the review process while keeping everyone on the same page. Google Docs with commenting features allow for real-time editing and feedback. Slack channels dedicated to content creation enable quick questions and approvals. Project management platforms like Trello or Asana help track content through various stages from ideation to publication. The key is creating transparent systems where contributors know exactly where to find assets, guidelines, and feedback—eliminating version control nightmares and last-minute scrambles.

Working with external creators requires special attention to brand alignment. Instead of rigid scripts, provide clear creative briefs that outline your goals, audience, and key messages while leaving room for their expertise. Establish a review process that catches inconsistencies early—perhaps requiring outlines or rough drafts before full production begins. Compensation should account for any revisions needed to meet brand standards, ensuring quality without stifling creativity.

Training is an ongoing process, not a one-time event. Regular workshops help both new and experienced contributors refine their understanding of your brand voice. Analyze past content together—what pieces best embodied your brand? Which ones missed the mark? Create a shared repository of "gold standard" examples that everyone can reference. Consider quarterly voice audits where you review recent content to identify any creeping inconsistencies.

The most successful content teams balance guidelines with creative freedom. Rather than dictating every word, focus on guarding the non-negotiables—core messaging, values, and audience needs—while allowing flexibility in how these are expressed. This approach maintains consistency while preventing your content from becoming stale or formulaic.

Practical Exercise:
Develop a mini style guide section covering:

1. Three core personality traits for your brand

2. Writing samples showing the right/wrong tone

3. Visual examples of on-brand/off-brand imagery
   This exercise helps you think critically about what makes your content uniquely yours—and how to communicate those standards to others.

Remember: Strong collaboration systems don't limit creativity — they channel it in directions that serve both your brand and your audience. When everyone understands and embraces your content standards, you create a multiplier effect where the whole becomes greater than the sum of its parts.

Exercise: Designing a Two-Week Editorial Calendar

Campaign Theme: "Small Business Productivity Boost"
Target Audience: Entrepreneurs and small business owners
Primary Goal: Increase engagement and website traffic
Secondary Goal: Grow email subscriber list

Week 1 Content Plan

Monday:

- **Platform:** Blog

- **Content Type:** Ultimate guide "5 Time Management Hacks for Busy Entrepreneurs"

- **Supporting Assets:** Custom infographic

- **Distribution:**

  o   LinkedIn: Post with key statistic from guide

  o   Twitter: Thread summarizing each hack

  o   Email: Excerpt to newsletter subscribers with full article link

Tuesday:

- **Platform:** Instagram

- **Content Type:** Carousel post "What's Wasting Your Time? (And How to Fix It)"

- **Supporting Assets:** Behind-the-scenes video of team testing productivity methods

- **Distribution:**

  o Instagram Stories: Poll about biggest time wasters

  o Pinterest: Infographic version

Wednesday:

- **Platform:** Email

- **Content Type:** Curated resources newsletter "Our Team's Favorite Productivity Tools"

- **Supporting Assets:** Downloadable comparison chart

- **Distribution:**

  o LinkedIn: Post about one featured tool

  o Twitter: Share tool recommendations

Thursday:

- **Platform:** Twitter

- **Content Type:** Twitter Spaces live discussion "Productivity Q&A with Experts"

- **Supporting Assets:** Blog post recap of key takeaways

- **Distribution:**

  o All channels: Promote in advance

  o Email: Send recording to subscribers

Friday:

- **Platform:** Blog

- **Content Type:** Case study "How Local Bakery Regained 10 Weekly Hours"

- **Supporting Assets:** Short customer testimonial video

- **Distribution:**

  o Facebook: Video snippet

  o LinkedIn: Detailed post about implementation

Week 2 Content Plan

Monday:

- **Platform:** LinkedIn

- **Content Type:** Article "The Psychology of Productivity: Why We Procrastinate"

- **Supporting Assets:** Psychological study references

- **Distribution:**

  o Twitter: Key findings thread

  o Email: Deep dive for subscribers

Tuesday:

- **Platform:** Instagram

- **Content Type:** Reel "1-Minute Productivity Tricks"

- **Supporting Assets:** Blog post with extended tips

- **Distribution:**

o TikTok: Adapted version

o Pinterest: Static image tips

Wednesday:

- **Platform:** Email

- **Content Type:** Challenge "3-Day Productivity Reset"

- **Supporting Assets:** Printable checklist

- **Distribution:**

o Social media: Daily reminder posts

Thursday:

- **Platform:** Twitter

- **Content Type:** Poll "What's Your Biggest Productivity Struggle?"

- **Supporting Assets:** Blog post addressing top answers

- **Distribution:**

o LinkedIn: Discussion post

Friday:

- **Platform:** Blog

- **Content Type:** Roundup "Your Productivity Questions Answered"

- **Supporting Assets:** Instagram Live recap

- **Distribution:**

  o All channels: Summary graphics

Key Features of This Calendar:

1. **Content Mix:** Balances educational (60%), interactive (20%), and promotional (20%) content

2. **Repurposing:** Core assets are adapted for multiple platforms

3. **Engagement Flow:** Starts with education, moves to interaction, concludes with CTA

4. **Measurement Plan:** Track blog traffic, social engagement, and email signups

Pro Tip: Use color-coding in your actual calendar to quickly identify content types (blue for blogs, green for social, etc.) and schedule preparation time for each piece.

Module 4: Measuring Performance and Optimization

Here's the hard truth about content marketing: if you're not measuring, you're just guessing.

All the creative ideas, beautifully crafted messages, and strategic distribution in the world won't matter if you can't prove what's actually working. This module is where we move from assumptions to evidence—where data transforms your content from good to high-performing.

Think of this as your content marketing health check. We'll start by identifying the vital signs (Lesson 1)—the key metrics that separate vanity numbers from meaningful indicators of success. Page views might stroke your ego, but are they leading to real business results? We'll focus on the measurements that actually matter.

Then we'll explore the diagnostic tools (Lesson 2)—Google Analytics, Hotjar, and platform insights that reveal how people interact with your content. These aren't just dashboards filled with numbers; they're treasure maps showing you exactly where to dig for opportunities. You'll learn which numbers to watch closely and which to ignore.

Finally, we'll get into the improvement cycle (Lesson 3)—using A/B testing and content analysis to make everything you publish work harder. You'll discover how small tweaks to headlines, layouts, or calls-to-action can lead to big jumps in performance. We'll also examine the different care required for evergreen content versus time-sensitive pieces.

The evaluation task will have you playing content doctor — diagnosing what's ailing one of your existing pieces and prescribing specific improvements. This hands-on analysis is where theory meets reality, helping you develop the critical eye that separates adequate content from exceptional content.

Here's what no one tells you: Optimization isn't a one-time fix — it's a mindset. The best content marketers aren't just creators; they're scientists who form hypotheses, test variables, and double down on what works. By the end of this module, you'll have that analytical approach wired into how you plan, create, and refine every piece of content.

Ready to stop guessing and start knowing? Let's measure what matters.

Lesson 1: Key Content Success Metrics

Numbers don't lie - but only if you're looking at the right ones. In content marketing, what gets measured gets improved, and understanding these metrics separates professionals from amateurs. Let's break down the three most revealing indicators of content performance and what they really tell you about your marketing effectiveness.

Views represent the most basic metric - how many people saw your content. While often dismissed as a vanity metric, views matter because they measure your content's reach and discoverability. High view counts on blog posts indicate strong SEO performance or effective social sharing. For videos, view counts show whether your thumbnails and titles compel clicks. But views alone don't tell the whole story - a piece could go viral while completely missing your target audience. The key is analyzing views in context: where they came from (organic search vs social referrals), who viewed them (demographics matching your personas), and what they did next. Sudden spikes in views might reveal what topics resonate during specific periods, helping you plan future content. Consistently low views signal either poor distribution or content that fails to connect with audience needs. The most valuable view metrics compare performance across similar content types - how does this video's views compare to others in the same series? This relative performance matters more than absolute numbers.

Time on page provides the crucial context views lack - not just whether people arrived, but whether they stayed. This metric reveals content quality and relevance more accurately than any other. For blog posts, industry benchmarks suggest 2-3 minutes as decent engagement, with under 1 minute indicating visitors quickly bounced. Video watch time percentages show whether you're hooking viewers or losing them early. The most revealing analysis comes from comparing time on page to content length - if readers spend 4 minutes on a 2000-word article, they're likely skimming rather than fully engaging. Time metrics also expose where you're losing readers - heatmaps might show people dropping off after your introduction or before your call-to-action. High time-on-page combined with low conversion rates suggests engaging content that fails to guide readers toward the next step. The most valuable content often shows a bimodal distribution - some readers skim quickly while others spend significant time, indicating both casual browsers and highly engaged prospects.

Conversion rates measure what ultimately matters - content's ability to drive meaningful actions. These could include email signups, content downloads, free trial starts, or direct purchases. Conversion metrics force you to define what "success" means for each piece of content - not all content should drive immediate sales, but all should move readers closer to becoming customers. Micro-conversions like comments or shares indicate engagement that may lead to macro-conversions later. The most sophisticated analysis tracks conversion paths - how many touchpoints a visitor needs before converting, and which content pieces most often appear in those paths. Surprisingly, some high-traffic content converts poorly while lower-traffic pieces drive disproportionate conversions - revealing your true high-value assets. Conversion rate optimization (CRO) for content involves testing different calls-to-action, placement strategies, and content upgrades to maximize this metric without compromising user experience.

The magic happens when you analyze these metrics together. A piece with high views but low time-on-page needs better audience targeting or more compelling introductions. Content with strong engagement but poor conversions may lack clear next steps. High-converting content with low views deserves promotion priority. This triangulation reveals your content's true performance beyond surface-level numbers.

Behavioral metrics add deeper context to these fundamentals. Scroll depth shows how far readers progress - are they reaching your key points? Click patterns reveal what links or elements attract attention. Video drop-off points indicate when you're losing viewers. These behavioral signals help optimize content structure and flow beyond just the raw numbers.

Engagement metrics provide qualitative insights to complement quantitative data. Comments, shares, and saves indicate emotional resonance - content that sparks conversation or gets bookmarked for later. High engagement often predicts long-term value even when immediate conversions seem low, as these pieces build relationships that pay off over time.

Return visitor rates measure content's ability to create loyal followers. While some content attracts one-time traffic, your most valuable pieces turn casual visitors into regular readers. Tracking how many visitors return after their first view helps identify content that builds lasting audience relationships rather than just generating hits.

Content attribution has become increasingly sophisticated. Multi-touch models reveal how different content pieces work together across the buyer's journey, rather than just crediting the final touchpoint. This helps justify ongoing investment in top-of-funnel content that nurtures leads even when it doesn't directly convert them.

Seasonal patterns emerge when analyzing metrics over time. Some content performs consistently while other pieces spike during specific periods. Recognizing these patterns allows for strategic content recycling and timely updates to capitalize on predictable interest surges.

The most effective content marketers don't just track metrics - they understand the stories behind the numbers. They know when a low view count reflects poor distribution versus unappealing content. They recognize when high time-on-page indicates deep engagement versus reader confusion. They appreciate how conversion rates vary appropriately across different content types and funnel stages. This nuanced understanding transforms raw data into actionable insights.

Segmenting metrics by traffic source provides particularly valuable insights. Organic search visitors often behave differently from social referrals - they may spend more time reading but convert at lower rates. Email subscribers typically show higher engagement than casual visitors. Understanding these differences helps tailor content and calls-to-action for each audience segment.

Device breakdowns reveal important usage patterns. Mobile visitors might consume content differently than desktop users - perhaps preferring shorter paragraphs or more visual elements. Significant discrepancies in metrics across devices signal opportunities for optimization to better serve each platform.

Content decay is an inevitable reality metrics help identify. Even evergreen pieces eventually lose traction as information becomes outdated or search algorithms change. Monitoring gradual declines in views, engagement, or conversions helps determine when content needs refreshing versus retirement.

The most valuable metric analysis compares performance against your specific goals rather than generic benchmarks. A "low" time-on-page might be excellent for quick-reference content, while a "high" conversion rate could still fall short of business needs. Context determines whether numbers indicate success or room for improvement.

Practical Exercise:
Choose three pieces of your existing content and analyze:

1. How view sources correlate with time spent

2. Where engagement peaks and drops off

3. What conversion paths emerge
   This exercise builds your ability to extract meaningful insights from raw metrics.

Remember: Metrics shouldn't stifle creativity - they should inform it. The numbers tell you what's working so you can do more of it, and what's not so you can adapt. When you master content metrics, every piece you create becomes an opportunity to learn and improve, creating a virtuous cycle of increasingly effective marketing.

Lesson 2: Analytics Tools

Data is only as valuable as your ability to interpret it, and that's where analytics tools become indispensable. These platforms transform raw numbers into actionable insights, helping you understand not just what's happening with your content, but why it's happening and how to improve. The right tools remove guesswork from content marketing, revealing exactly how audiences discover, consume, and engage with your material across different channels.

Google Analytics serves as the foundational tool for content performance measurement, offering unparalleled depth for website content analysis. The platform's behavior reports show which pages attract and retain visitors, while acquisition reports reveal how people find your content in the first place. The real power comes from setting up custom dashboards that focus specifically on content metrics - bounce rates for blog posts, average session duration for different content categories, and goal completions tied to content downloads or newsletter signups. The Page Value metric helps identify which content pieces contribute most to conversions, even if they aren't the final landing pages. Setting up content grouping allows you to compare performance across different types of material - seeing how long-form guides stack up against quick tips or video transcripts. The Audience Reports provide demographic and interest data that helps refine your content strategy to better match your visitor profiles. Custom segments let you isolate and analyze specific visitor groups - comparing new versus returning readers, or organic search visitors versus social referrals.

Hotjar complements Google Analytics by showing the human behavior behind the numbers through heatmaps and session recordings. Heatmaps visually represent where visitors click, how far they scroll, and what they ignore - revealing whether key content elements actually get seen. For blog content, heatmaps often show whether visitors reach your calls-to-action or bounce before scrolling past the introduction. Session recordings provide play-by-play views of individual visits, showing exactly how real people navigate your content - where they pause, what links they click, and where they encounter confusion. The tool's feedback widgets allow direct input from visitors through polls and surveys, asking what information they came looking for or why they're leaving. Form analysis helps optimize content upgrades and lead capture elements by showing where visitors drop off in the signup process. Hotjar's coming-from and going-to reports reveal the paths visitors take through your content, helping identify logical sequences and gaps in your content architecture.

Social Media Insights tools built into each platform provide specialized metrics for content shared outside your website. Facebook's Page Insights shows reach, engagement, and follower demographics for shared content, along with when your audience is most active. Instagram Insights reveals which types of posts (stories, reels, grid posts) generate the most profile visits and follows. Twitter Analytics highlights which tweets drive the most clicks, retweets, and replies. LinkedIn's analytics dashboard shows content-specific demographics including job titles and industries of engaged viewers. Each platform's native analytics help determine optimal posting times, content formats, and messaging styles that resonate with your specific audience on that channel. The key is looking beyond vanity metrics like likes - focusing instead on saves, shares, and click-through rates that indicate deeper engagement. Hashtag performance reports help refine your content tagging strategy to increase discoverability. Follower growth analytics tied to specific content pieces reveal which topics attract new audience members versus just engaging existing followers.

The most effective content marketers use these tools in combination rather than isolation. Google Analytics might show a blog post has high traffic but low time-on-page, Hotjar reveals visitors aren't scrolling past the first screen, and social insights indicate the shared link receives few clicks - together pointing to a weak introduction that needs optimization. This triangulation of data sources provides the complete picture needed for meaningful improvements.

Setting up proper tracking is essential before collecting data. Google Analytics requires proper implementation of tracking codes and goal configurations. Hotjar needs careful selection of which pages to record based on traffic volume and importance. Social media insights often require switching to professional/business accounts. Taking time to configure these tools correctly ensures the data you collect will be accurate and actionable rather than misleading.

Custom reporting saves time while focusing attention on the metrics that matter most. Google Analytics custom reports can combine acquisition, behavior, and conversion metrics for content in one view. Social platforms allow saving frequently used report filters. Dashboards that pull key metrics from multiple sources into one view help spot trends and correlations that individual tools might miss. Automated report delivery ensures stakeholders stay informed without manual effort.

Annotation features in these tools help track changes and correlate them with performance shifts. Noting when you published a major content piece or changed your social media strategy creates reference points in your analytics timeline. This practice helps distinguish organic trends from the impact of specific actions, making it clearer what's actually driving results.

Comparative analysis periods reveal what's improving versus declining. Comparing this month's content metrics to last month's or year-over-year performance shows whether changes are moving the needle. Seasonality adjustments help account for normal fluctuations unrelated to content quality or strategy.

Segmentation unlocks deeper insights than aggregate numbers alone. Analyzing how different audience groups interact with your content - by age, location, device, or traffic source - reveals opportunities to better tailor your material. Seeing that mobile visitors convert at half the rate of desktop users might prompt a mobile-first content redesign. Discovering that LinkedIn referrals spend twice as long on pages as Twitter referrals could influence your distribution priorities.

Event tracking takes measurement beyond page views to specific content interactions. Tracking video plays, PDF downloads, or interactive tool usage provides a fuller picture of engagement. These micro-conversions often indicate high intent that precedes macro-conversions like purchases or lead submissions.

Content grouping allows analysis by theme or format rather than just individual pieces. Comparing how all "how-to" articles perform versus "case studies" or "opinion pieces" reveals what content approaches resonate best with your audience. This higher-level analysis helps guide broader content strategy decisions beyond just optimizing individual posts.

Alerts and anomalies detection spot opportunities or issues quickly. Setting up custom alerts for traffic spikes or conversion rate drops ensures you notice and respond to significant changes. Sudden ranking improvements might indicate content worth doubling down on, while unexpected declines could signal technical issues or algorithm changes affecting your visibility.

Integrations between these tools create powerful workflows. Connecting Google Analytics with Google Search Console provides richer SEO performance data. Hotjar recordings can be filtered by Google Analytics segments to study specific visitor groups. Social media management tools often incorporate native analytics while adding cross-platform comparison capabilities. These connections help break down data silos for more holistic insights.

The true art lies in interpreting data patterns rather than just collecting numbers. A high bounce rate might indicate irrelevant traffic - or it might mean visitors found exactly what they needed quickly. Increased time-on-page could signal engaging content - or confusing navigation that frustrates visitors. Social shares might reflect thought leadership - or controversial takes that don't actually drive business results. Context and business objectives determine whether metrics represent success or warning signs.

Practical Exercise:

Install and configure basic tracking in one analytics tool. Create a simple dashboard with three key content metrics and analyze one week's worth of data to identify:

1. Your best-performing content piece

2. Your most engaged audience segment

3. One opportunity for improvement
   This hands-on experience builds comfort with data interpretation that no theoretical study can match.

Remember: Analytics tools are means to an end, not the end itself. The goal isn't to collect data, but to uncover insights that inform better content decisions. When used thoughtfully, these tools become compasses that keep your content strategy aligned with real audience needs and behaviors rather than guesses or assumptions. The marketers who master analytics don't just create content - they create content that provably works.

Lesson 3: Continuous Improvement

The difference between good content and great content often comes down to one crucial mindset: the commitment to never stop improving. In the fast-evolving digital landscape, what worked yesterday might underperform tomorrow, making continuous optimization not just beneficial but essential. This lesson explores two powerful approaches to keep your content strategy fresh and effective - the scientific precision of A/B testing and the strategic balance between evergreen and time-sensitive content.

A/B testing transforms content improvements from guesswork to data-driven decisions. Also known as split testing, this method involves creating two versions of a content element with a single key difference, then measuring which version performs better with your audience. The elements worth testing range from obvious candidates like headlines and call-to-action buttons to more subtle factors like image placement, paragraph length, or even color schemes. For email content, you might test subject lines against each other to see which generates higher open rates. On landing pages, you could experiment with different hero images to determine which drives more conversions. The key to effective A/B testing lies in isolating variables - testing one change at a time to clearly attribute any performance differences to that specific modification. Testing duration matters too - running tests long enough to gather statistically significant data while avoiding seasonal anomalies that could skew results. Modern tools like Google Optimize or specialized WordPress plugins make setting up these tests surprisingly simple, often requiring no technical expertise. The real value comes from systematically applying these learnings across your content portfolio - when you discover that question headlines outperform statement headlines in tests, you can apply that insight to future content creation.

Evergreen content represents the foundation of a sustainable content strategy - material that remains relevant and valuable long after publication. These cornerstone pieces address fundamental questions in your industry, explain timeless principles, or provide comprehensive guides to perennial challenges. A financial advisor's "Beginner's Guide to Retirement Planning" or a software company's "Ultimate Glossary of Coding Terms" exemplify evergreen content that attracts consistent traffic over months and years. The strength of evergreen content lies in its compounding returns - well-optimized pieces continue working for your business with minimal maintenance. However, evergreen doesn't mean "create once and forget." These pieces require periodic updates to refresh statistics, incorporate new examples, and maintain their search rankings. A smart practice involves scheduling evergreen content audits every 6-12 months to ensure accuracy and relevance. Evergreen content particularly shines for organic search strategies, as these pieces have time to climb search rankings and establish authority. They also serve as ideal candidates for content upgrades - lead magnets that convert casual readers into email subscribers by offering expanded or specialized versions of the free content.

Time-sensitive content captures attention by riding waves of immediate interest. This category includes news reactions, trend analyses, holiday-themed pieces, and commentary on current industry developments. A marketing agency analyzing the implications of a major algorithm update or a retailer creating "Back-to-School Essentials" guides exemplify timely content. The advantage lies in the built-in urgency and relevance - audiences actively searching for these topics right now. Social platforms particularly favor this fresh content, often boosting visibility for topics generating current discussion. The challenge comes in the limited shelf life - what's relevant today may be forgotten next week. Production speed becomes crucial with time-sensitive content, requiring streamlined workflows to capitalize on fleeting opportunities. Savvy marketers balance this by creating templates and frameworks that can be quickly adapted when timely topics emerge. Another smart approach involves adding evergreen elements to time-sensitive pieces - a post about "2024 Tax Changes" could include a section on "Timeless Tax Planning Principles" that maintains value beyond the current year.

The most effective content strategies intelligently blend both approaches. Evergreen content provides the stable foundation that drives consistent traffic and leads, while timely pieces capitalize on current opportunities to boost visibility and engagement. A common ratio involves allocating about 70% of resources to evergreen creation and 30% to timely content, though this varies by industry and audience. The blend also depends on your sales cycle - businesses with longer consideration periods may emphasize evergreen content that nurtures leads over time, while impulse-driven markets might prioritize timely promotions.

Content decay analysis helps determine when and how to update existing material. Even the best evergreen content eventually shows signs of declining performance - dropping search rankings, decreasing engagement metrics, or outdated information. Regular reviews of your content portfolio identify which pieces need refreshing, which should be retired, and which continue performing well. Updating successful evergreen content often proves more efficient than creating net-new pieces, as you build upon existing authority rather than starting from scratch. The process involves both content revisions (updating statistics, refreshing examples) and technical optimizations (improving meta descriptions, adding internal links).

Multivariate testing takes optimization beyond simple A/B tests by examining how multiple variables interact. While more complex to set up and interpret, these tests can reveal powerful combinations - perhaps a specific headline style works best with short introductory paragraphs but fails with longer ones. This sophisticated approach works best after establishing baseline performance through simpler A/B tests.

Personalization represents the next frontier of content optimization. Advanced tools now allow dynamic content that adapts based on viewer characteristics - showing different examples to beginners versus experts, or highlighting relevant products based on past behavior. While requiring more technical implementation, personalization can dramatically improve engagement and conversion rates by delivering precisely what each visitor needs.

Predictive analytics are beginning to transform content optimization. AI tools can analyze past performance data to suggest which topics, formats, and distribution strategies will likely resonate best with your audience. These insights help prioritize content initiatives with the highest probable return on investment.

The content improvement cycle never truly ends - each optimization provides new data that informs the next round of refinements. This continuous process might involve quarterly content audits, monthly A/B tests, and weekly performance reviews. The goal isn't perfection but progressive improvement - making each piece slightly better than the last, and each campaign more effective than the previous one.

Practical Exercise:

Select one piece of existing content and:

1. Identify one element to A/B test (headline, image, etc.)

2. Outline how you would adapt it for both evergreen and timely versions

3. Propose three specific optimizations based on performance   data
    This exercise builds the improvement mindset that distinguishes professional content marketers.

Remember: Continuous improvement in content marketing isn't about constant churn or chasing every new trend. It's about developing systematic approaches to learn from every piece you publish, applying those lessons to future work, and maintaining the right balance between timeless value and timely relevance. When you institutionalize this improvement mindset, your content strategy becomes a self-refining engine that grows more effective over time.

Evaluation Task: Content Performance Analysis & Improvement Plan

Selected Content Piece:

"7 Time Management Hacks for Busy Entrepreneurs" (Blog post published 3 months ago)

Performance Analysis

Traffic Metrics:

- Total views: 2,450 (42% organic search, 28% social, 20% email, 10% direct)

- Average time on page: 1 min 45 sec (compared to site average of 2 min 30 sec)

- Bounce rate: 68% (higher than site average of 58%)

Engagement Metrics:

- Social shares: 89 (primarily LinkedIn and Twitter)

- Comments: 12 (mostly asking follow-up questions)

- Email click-through rate: 3.2% (when included in newsletter)

Conversion Metrics:

- Content upgrade downloads: 47 (2% conversion rate)

- Subsequent page views: 32% of visitors viewed another post

- Lead form submissions: 9 (0.4% conversion rate)

Heatmap Observations:

- 60% of visitors don't scroll past the first screen

- Most clicks occur on the first two tips

- Content upgrade CTA gets minimal engagement

Improvement Opportunities

1. Content Structure Optimization

- Problem: High bounce rate and low scroll depth indicate weak introduction

- Solution:

  o Rewrite opening to immediately address reader pain points

  o Add "What to Expect" preview box listing key benefits

  o Move one compelling hack above the fold as a teaser

  o Break up long paragraphs with more subheadings

2. Visual Enhancement

- Problem: Text-heavy format fails to engage visual learners

- Solution:

  o Add custom illustrations for each time management hack

  o Include progress tracker showing reading time

  o Create infographic summary for social sharing

o   Embed short video clips demonstrating techniques

3. Conversion Pathway Improvements

- Problem: Low conversion rates despite decent traffic

- Solution:

o   Replace generic content upgrade with specific "Time Audit Template"

o   Add mid-content CTA after third hack

o   Test different anchor text for internal links

o   Include case study sidebar showing real results

4. SEO Optimization

- Problem: Declining organic traffic after initial spike

- Solution:

o   Refresh with 2024 statistics and examples

o   Add FAQ section targeting long-tail questions

o   Build 3-5 quality backlinks from industry resources

o   Update meta description with power words

5. Repurposing Strategy

- Problem: Single-use content wasting potential

- Solution:

o   Create Twitter thread breaking down each hack

- Film office hours session discussing implementations

- Develop podcast episode featuring entrepreneur case studies

- Compile into email course with daily challenges

Implementation Plan

Phase 1: Quick Wins (Week 1)

- Rewrite introduction and add subheadings

- Create basic infographic for social promotion

- Add time estimate progress tracker

Phase 2: Core Improvements (Week 2-3)

- Redesign content upgrade and CTAs

- Produce 2-3 demonstration videos

- Build FAQ section and refresh statistics

Phase 3: Repurposing (Ongoing)

- Launch Twitter thread series

- Schedule podcast recording

- Develop email course sequence

Measurement Plan:

- Track changes in:

- Time on page (target: +30 seconds)

- Scroll depth (target: 50% reach halfway point)

- Conversion rate (target: 4% for content upgrades)

- Organic search position (target: top 3 for main keyword)

Testing Approach:

- A/B test original vs. revised introduction

- Compare infographic vs. video versions on social

- Evaluate different CTA placements

This improvement plan focuses on enhancing engagement while maximizing return from existing content assets. The proposed changes address identified weaknesses while capitalizing on the post's demonstrated strengths in topic relevance and social sharing potential.

Capstone Project

Develop a complete content marketing strategy for a brand:

- Define the target audience

- Select content types

- Choose distribution channels

- Build a timeline

- Set measurement and evaluation methods

About the author

Dr. Aziza Tawfiq Abdelghafar, a PhD holder from Ain Shams University, is an expert in strategic planning, marketing, and administrative sciences. With extensive experience in academia, industry, and entrepreneurship, she has authored specialized books and research papers. A sought-after speaker, she has contributed to scientific and industrial conferences, shaping the future of marketing and management sciences.